Supernatural Joy

Alan Leonhardt

Supernatural Joy

Copyright © 2020 by Alan F. Leonhardt

All Rights Reserved. No part of this publication may be reproduced, stored in a retrieval system, or transmitted in any form or by any means - for example, electronic, photocopy, and recording - without the prior written permission of the publisher. The only exception is brief quotations in printed reviews.

Published by Lionheart Publications,
a division of Lionheart Ministries
1600 W. State Rd
Hastings, MI 49058
alanleonhardt@gmail.com

Unless otherwise indicated, scripture quotations are taken from the New King James Version. Copyright © 1982 Thomas Nelson, Inc. Used by permission. All rights reserved.

Scripture quotations marked NIV are taken from the Holy Bible, New International Version Copyright © 1973, 1978, 1984 by International Bible Society. Used by permission of Zondervan. All rights reserved.

Scripture quotations marked AMP are taken from the Amplified Bible. Copyright © 1954, 1958, 1962, 1964, 1965, 1987 by the Lockman Foundation. Used by permission.

Cover design, editing, and interior design by Kathy Mayo

ISBNs: 978-1-7348354-2-7 (printed) 978-1-7348354-3-4 (ebook)
First edition: May 2020

Printed in the United States of America

Previous Books by Alan Leonhardt

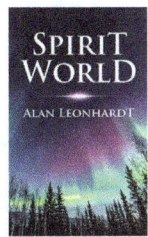

Spirit World, 2019

There is a deep spiritual side to the Christian experience. In this book, Dr Leonhardt relates his own personal journey with dreams, visions, hearing from God, speaking in tongues, and other powerful gifts of the Holy Spirit.

Pathway to Promotion, 2020

God has a destiny for every believer. He wants to bless you exceedingly, abundantly and above your wildest dreams. As we cooperate with God's principles for advancement, we will break out of a mediocre Christian life and find the Pathway to Promotion.

Dedication

I want to dedicate my all books to my wife Nicole, my four beautiful daughters, and the next generation.

> *One generation shall praise Your works to another,*
> *And shall declare Your mighty acts.*
> *~ Psalm 145:4*

We have an obligation to pass on our wisdom and experience to the next generation. My biggest inspirations are my children. I want my ceiling in life to be their starting place and platform.

If we are wise, we will admit that we all stand on the shoulders of great men and women who have mentored us with the sacrifice of their lives. If someone can glean any good thing from my books that will help establish them and give them greater endurance to finish their race, then I will have done my job.

Contents

Introduction ... 7

Hope is the Foundation ... 11

   Day 1
      The God of Hope ... 12

   Day 2
      Hope Deferred ... 15

   Day 3
      Hope is the Anchor of the Soul ... 18

   Day 4
      Prisoners of Hope ... 21

   Day 5
      Hope in God's Word ... 24

   Day 6
      There is Hope in Your Future ... 27

   Day 7
      Your Future Looks Good ... 30

Supernatural Joy ... 33

   Day 8
      The Oil of Joy ... 34

   Day 9
      God's Favor Brings Joy ... 38

   Day 10
      Joy is Found in Giving ... 41

   Day 11
      There is Joy in God's Presence ... 43

Day 12
   Ask, That Your Joy May Be Full 46

Day 13
   God Rejoices Over You 48

Day 14
   Joy Comes in the Morning 52

Holy Laughter 55

Day 15
   He Causes Laughter 56

Day 16
   He Fills Your Mouth With Laughter 58

Day 17
   Laughing is Intercession 60

Day 18
   Laughter is Healing 63

Day 19
   Laughter is Victory 65

Day 20
   Obedience Brings Joy 67

Day 21
   Praying in the Spirit 70

How to Know God Personally 73

Introduction

This book was born out of the crucible of experience. People say that experience is the best teacher. I wish it wasn't so because experience can be a cruel taskmaster.

People who know me would classify me as a sanguine personality; confident, outgoing, always looking for the punch line as I look at the lighter side of things. There is another side to me that most do not see. A hidden melancholy man; bookish, pensive, with a tendency to be a perfectionist. I push him down and keep him under control. He is part of me and I don't want to kill him; he makes me a more thoughtful creative person. But I cannot let him dominate; when he does it leads to a dark night of the soul. In the dark land of shadows, demons, and death, I have reached for help that was beyond me. I didn't have the strength of will within to overcome on my own. I cried out to God and He showed me how to access His supernatural joy. He taught me how to overcome despair and be filled with fresh hope, joy, and laughter. You may think I am being dramatic, but those who have been vexed with a spirit of despondency and hopelessness know what an oppressive killer it can be.

Beloved, I pray that you may prosper in all things and be in health, just as your soul prospers. For I rejoiced greatly when brethren came and testified of the truth that is in you, just as you walk in the truth. I have no greater joy than to hear that my children walk in truth.
~ III John 1:2-4

The most important thing in our lives is the prosperity of the soul. It affects all aspects of this precious life that God has given us. If our soul is illuminated with the eternal truth of God's promises, then we will be filled with hope and joy. The truth always brings hope. Lies always bring hopelessness. If we are hopeless, we are believing a lie. The Holy Spirit wants to expose that lie and renew your mind.

> *But the path of the just is like the shining sun,*
> *that shines ever brighter unto the perfect day.*
> *~ Proverbs 4:18*

As we embrace the light and truth that God gives us, more will be given to us. Some healings are instantaneous, and some are gradual. At times, the presence of God in a church service can bring a flood of joy and laughter. But life's pain isn't always repaired in an instant. A miracle is instantaneous, a healing happens gradually over time. You need to develop a lifestyle of reaching for God's abundant supply of joy. You must create new pathways in your thinking; a discernment that learns to reject hopeless lies and embrace hope, light, and truth.

In the book you have in your hands, I have given you some great tools on your journey to living the abundant life that Jesus promised (see John 10:10). It will take 21 days for you to develop new pathways of thinking. Doing something consistently for 21 days develops a new habit. New habits form into a lifestyle. You are about to develop a lifestyle of joy.

This book is designed in three parts:

Hope is the Foundation: Without hope you cannot have lasting joy. What is biblical hope? How can I increase my hopefulness? If you have hoped for something only to be disappointed, you can refocus your hope. You can overcome and move forward to victory.

Introduction

Supernatural Joy: The joy that comes from God is not just an inner sense of wellbeing. It is a spiritual strength that is indestructible. Once you have the foundation of hope set in place, you can begin to access supernatural joy.

Holy Laughter: "He will yet fill your mouth with laughing, And your lips with rejoicing." (Job 8:21). There will be times when God's supernatural joy manifests in a belly laugh. When is the last time you had a good laugh? Once you have experienced healing laughter, you will be able to access it again. Learn the purpose of laughing in the spirit.

It's my prayer that this book blesses you greatly and sets you on a trajectory for success. There is a joy that can be accessed that is beyond human capacity to describe; it's unspeakable and full of glory. Amen

*Whom having not seen you love. Though now you
do not see Him, yet believing, you rejoice
with joy inexpressible and full of glory.
~ I Peter 1:8*

Pastor Alan Leonhardt D.Th

HOPE IS THE FOUNDATION

*Now may the God of hope
fill you with all joy and
peace in believing,
that you may abound in
hope by the power of
the Holy Spirit.
~ Romans 15:13*

Day 1

The God of Hope

*Now may the God of hope fill you with all joy and peace in believing, that **you may abound in hope** by the power of the Holy Spirit.*
~ Romans 15:13

A thick heavy blanket descended upon my life. That's one of the ways I can describe it. The despondency had weight to it. It pressed down on me and zapped me of all my energy and vitality. I know what it's like to despair even of life itself.

I was in Bible College at the time and was working full time as a cook in a restaurant. I shared a house with two roommates. The perfect emotional storm was buffeting my life. I was having problems with my church and had feelings of being disconnected. I felt stuck in a dead-end job. A girl I was quite fond of made known to me in no uncertain terms that a relationship beyond friendship was not going to happen. I was disconnected from my family for many reasons.

A romantic rejection is tough on its own, but it seemed that all the rejections of my life were now piling on top of my back. I had become the whipping boy for a powerful, oppressive, hulking, demonic spirit. I had lost all hope that anything good would come my way. I looked in the mirror and saw an ugly person who would never achieve his dreams. Dreams just seemed like fantasies that give false hope; an illusion that can never really be attained, but were a cruel trick to get us to endure the hellscape that was the reality of life. I was entertaining thoughts of suicide. The heaviness was so overwhelming at times, that late at night I would call a friend and make him talk to me because I was afraid I might kill myself.

In the midst of this vicious cycle of despondency and hopelessness, I was somehow led to the scripture above, Romans 15:13. The Holy Spirit began to put me through a kind of personal therapy program. I wish I could tell you that I had a miraculous encounter so powerful that all depression and hopelessness instantly vanished, but that wasn't the case. Let me break down for you this victorious verse and show you how the Holy Spirit, that great teacher and counselor, helped me climb out of a lifestyle of melancholy.

1. "*Now may the God of **hope**...*"

Hope is seeing **good things** in your life and future. Having hope is **the key** to living in supernatural joy. Hope comes from God; He is the "God of hope." He is the source and fountainhead of a never-ending artesian well springing with hope. The Hope that comes from God is not wishful thinking. It's not like when people say, "I hope so." God gives a realistic hope. An attainable hope.

2. "*...fill you with all joy and peace in **believing**...*"

You must start to **believe**; **believing** causes this supernatural hope to fill you. You have to start changing how you think. Whatever doesn't bring hope is not of God. When hopeless thinking starts flooding your mind, you must raise up a standard of faith against it. When you bring a mustard seed portion of **faith** to the table, and start seeing good in your future, God almighty answers with hope, joy, and peace. It starts with you beginning to **believe** again.

> *I would have lost heart, unless I had believed that I would see the goodness of the Lord in the land of the living. Wait on the Lord; Be of good courage, and He shall*

> *strengthen your heart; Wait, I say, on the Lord!*
> *~ Psalm 27:13-14*

3. "*...that you may abound in hope by the power of the Holy Spirit.*"

When you start to **believe** and hope again, the power of the Holy Spirit kicks in, and abounding hope lights the darkness of your soul. This is a partnership. You have to bring something to the table. God is working with you (see Mark 16:20). Draw near to God and He will draw near to you (see James 4:8). Take those daily steps of **believing** and your hope level will begin to rise. As your hope level rises, your joy level will rise too.

As you read these devotionals day by day, you will begin to make new pathways in your thinking. Instead of automatically taking the hopeless path, you will take the path of faith, hope, and love. God has amazing things for you. Your future looks good. It's so awesome that your finite mind cannot comprehend the endless expanse of God's goodness.

> *But as it is written: "Eye has not seen, nor ear heard, nor have entered into the heart of man the things which God has prepared for those who love Him."*
> *~ I Corinthians 2:9*

> *Now to Him who is able to do exceedingly abundantly above all that we ask or think, according to the power that works in us, to Him be glory in the church by Christ Jesus to all generations, forever and ever. Amen.*
> *~ Ephesians 3:20-21*

Dear Heavenly Father,

Today I will begin a journey of hope and joy. I will renew my mind to Your promises and the hope that comes from You. I will begin to reject negative thoughts. Whatever does not bring hope is not of You and therefore a lie. I will only listen to the encouragement of the Holy Spirit.

In Jesus' mighty name, Amen

Day 2

HOPE DEFERRED

*Hope deferred makes the heart sick, but when
the desire comes, it is a tree of life.
~ Proverbs 13:12*

We have all put our hope in something only to be let down. The greater the hope, the greater the disappointment. How we overcome these setbacks will inspire others.

Life has a way of punching you in the gut. Sometimes you believe you heard from God but things didn't work out. You go over and over in your mind how it all fell to pieces. You look for someone or something to blame. Sometimes the answer is simple, sometimes it's complicated, and sometimes there is no answer this side of heaven.

The prophet Samuel found himself in a hopeless situation. He had heard from God that Saul was to be the first King of Israel. Signs confirmed God's choice, spectacular signs and wonders (see 1 Samuel 9 & 10), and yet Saul was an epic failure. Finally, we find Samuel in a perpetual state of mourning for King Saul and the nation of Israel (see 1 Samuel 15:34-35).

I have known people to go through tremendous loss and never cycle out of the grieving process. A spiritual oppression of perpetual mourning attaches itself and they can't break free.

There would be no hope if it wasn't for the God of hope (see Romans 15:13). Only Jesus can help us crawl out a pit of heart sickness.

> ***To console those who mourn*** *in Zion, to give them **beauty for ashes**, the oil of **joy for mourning**, the garment of praise for the spirit of heaviness; that they may be called trees of righteousness, the planting of the Lord, that He may be glorified. The Spirit of the Lord God is upon Me, because the Lord has anointed Me to preach good tidings to the poor; He has sent Me to **heal the brokenhearted**, to proclaim liberty to the captives, and the opening of the prison to those who are bound; to proclaim the acceptable year of the Lord , and the day of vengeance of our God; to **comfort all who mourn.***
> ~ *Isaiah 61:1-3*

God spoke to Samuel and pulled him out of mourning. The word was very simple and straight forward; He told Samuel to fill his horn with oil and go anoint another replacement for Saul.

> *Now the Lord said to Samuel, "How long will you mourn for Saul, seeing I have rejected him from reigning over Israel? Fill your horn with oil, and go; I am sending you to Jesse the Bethlehemite. For I have provided Myself a king among his sons."*
> ~ *I Samuel 16:1*

At first glance, it seems insensitive of God to just tell Samuel to stop mourning and move on. There was no explanation for what went wrong. The answer was obvious; Saul's constant disobedience messed everything up. But wait, didn't God, in His vast foreknowledge, know that Saul would mess up? If God put Saul in a position of great influence knowing that he would fail, that would make God the author of failure and sin. God takes a chance on us; He encourages us and believes in us. We are not puppets on a string. Saul WAS God's choice, Samuel didn't mess up; Saul did. People make choices and sometimes those choices are poor ones. God has a backup plan when things go sideways. He is so awesome that His plan B can eventually work out better than plan A.

> *And we know that **all things** work together for good to those who love God, to those who are the called according to His purpose.*
> *~ Romans 8:28*

Nothing can work against you, but only for you. We live in a fallen world and sin happens. There can still be a victory achieved out of every setback and loss. 1 Samuel 16:1 is a prophetic word for you, "Go and anoint another." Move forward to the new thing. There will still be pain from the loss or failure, but you can rise above it. You can live again with fresh hope and joy. What new thing does God have for you to move forward in? I know my God. Seek Him and He will speak to you about refocusing your faith and hope on something or someone new.

> *Behold, the former things have come to pass, and new things I declare; Before they spring forth I tell you of them.*
> *~ Isaiah 42:9*

Make a commitment with me today that you will seek the Lord about the new things He has for you. Say this prayer with me:

Dear Father in heaven,

I turn my broken heart over to You today. Bring Your healing oil of joy and pour it into the wounds. I commit this day that with Your help I will hope again. I will seek You for the new things You have for me. I thank You in advance for speaking to my heart. Thank You for loving me and not giving up on me.
In Jesus' name, Amen

> *For You are my rock and my fortress; Therefore, for Your name's sake, lead me and guide me.*
> *~ Psalm 31:3*

Day 3

Hope is the Anchor of the Soul

Thus God, determining to show more abundantly to the heirs of promise the immutability of His counsel, confirmed it by an oath, that by two immutable things, in which it is impossible for God to lie, we might have strong consolation, who have fled for refuge to lay hold of the hope set before us.
This hope we have as an anchor of the soul*, both sure and steadfast, and which enters the Presence behind the veil.*
~ Hebrews 6:17-19

I needed saving from myself. My mind and emotions needed stability. When I came to God, He brought an anchor to my soul. Everything around us is always in a state of flux and change. Some change happens so fast that it can be traumatizing. But oh... the safety and security that God can bring. Being rooted, grounded, and established in God's love and Word brings strength and stability to an unstable soul. Imagine being trapped on a ship caught in a raging typhoon. After days of stormy seas, you begin to ask yourself, "Is this how the rest of my life is going to be? Constant fear, trauma, and instability?" You begin to lose all hope of a better life. Then the sun comes out, the sea stops its foaming upheaval, and you arrive at a sheltered haven.

THE IMMUTABILITY OF GOD'S COUNSEL

Immutability means unchangeable. God does not change. He is not evolving. He is perfect. He is all-knowing and all-powerful. He is and was, and always will be forever and ever. He is the center and stability of the universe. He is the source of creation and He upholds all things by the Word of His power (see Hebrews 1:3). He is transcendent of the universe. He does not need the universe to survive, the universe needs His powerful Word to sustain. Because He does not change, we have a safe port to which we can anchor our souls. He is the only real stable force in this life.

> *For I am the Lord, I do not change; therefore*
> *you are not consumed, O sons of Jacob.*
> *~ Malachi 3:6*

> *Jesus Christ is the same yesterday, today, and forever.*
> *~ Hebrews 13:8 NKJV*

IT IS IMPOSSIBLE FOR GOD TO LIE

Just think about the security this brings. It is against God's nature to ever lie to you. He will never make a promise that He cannot keep. And His promises will last forever. You're not going to get anything more stable than that. Build your life upon the rock of Jesus and His words. Let the moorings of your soul anchor deeply into the bedrock of God's unchangeable love.

> *For all the promises of God in Him are Yes, and in Him Amen,*
> *to the glory of God through us.*
> *~ II Corinthians 1:20*

> *God is not a man, that He should lie, nor a son of man, that*
> *He should repent. Has He said, and will He not do?*
> *Or has He spoken, and will He not make it good?*
> *~ Numbers 23:19*

> *Behold, this day I am going the way of all the earth. And you*
> *know in all your hearts and in all your souls that not one thing*
> *has failed of all the good things which the Lord your God*

> *spoke concerning you. All have come to pass
> for you; not one word of them has failed.*
> *~ Joshua 23:14*

> *The entirety of Your word is truth, and every one of
> Your righteous judgments endures forever.*
> *~ Psalm 119:160*

> *Heaven and earth will pass away, but My words
> will by no means pass away.*
> *~ Matthew 24:35*

YOU MUST HAVE AN ESTABLISHED HEART

An established heart is so grounded in God's word that it is not easily shaken by fearful reports. To have an unshakable hope means that we must be a person of the Word; a person who often reads and meditates on God's eternal promises.

> *He will not be afraid of evil tidings; His heart is steadfast,
> trusting in the Lord. His heart is established; He will not be
> afraid, until he sees his desire upon his enemies.*
> *~ Psalm 112:7-8*

God wants to minister to you today. He is assuring you that you are important to Him and you can securely trust Him. Say this prayer and release all fear of change. God's hope is the anchor of your soul.

Dear Heavenly Father,

Please forgive me for my fearfulness and lack of trust. I will not be so fearful of change from this day forward. I have been disappointed and heartbroken, but my hope is in You. You will deliver me out of all storms and into safe havens. You are my ultimate safe haven in this life. I love you Lord.

In Jesus' mighty name, Amen

> *For You are my hope, O Lord God;
> You are my trust from my youth.*
> *Psalm 71:5*

Day 4

PRISONERS OF HOPE

*As for you also, Because of the blood of your covenant, I will
set your prisoners free from the waterless pit.
Return to the stronghold, You prisoners of hope.
Even today I declare That I will restore double to you.
~ Zechariah 9:11-12*

I remember where I was when God renewed my call to ministry. I was sitting in a side pew looking out the window. I told God that I was quitting ministry. A family that I was close to started spreading rumors and stopped coming to church without a word. It felt like such a major betrayal. I didn't even know the full reason for their offense. I felt like such a failure. I figured if I had to deal with people coming and going in my life on a whim, I might as well own a business and make some money. That's when God spoke to me with this verse:

*O Lord, You are the portion of my inheritance and my cup;
You maintain my lot. The lines have fallen to me in pleasant
places; Yes, I have a good inheritance.
~ Psalm 16:5-6*

I wept in that pew because I knew what God was saying. He is my portion and inheritance. People may come and go but I have Him forever. My inheritance was ministry and that would never be taken away from me. I came into a new appreciation for my call into ministry. It was a great honor and a sacred trust.

I became a prisoner of hope. Hope heals hurt, betrayal, and failure. God's love and acceptance has captured me for life and I have a good inheritance.

Because of the blood of your covenant

If you are in Christ, a born-again Christian, you have a covenant by blood with God almighty. Jesus shed His precious blood on the cross. Without the shedding of blood, there is no remission of sins (see Hebrews 9:22, 1 Peter 1:18-19). Your sins are forgiven and cleansed. You are now the righteousness of God in Christ Jesus (see 2 Corinthians 5:21). You now qualify for all of the covenant promises of God (see Ephesians 2:12).

> *Then one of the elders answered, saying to me, "Who are these arrayed in white robes, and where did they come from?" And I said to him, "Sir, you know." So he said to me, "These are the ones who come out of the great tribulation, and washed their robes and made them white in the blood of the Lamb."*
> *~ Revelation 7:13-14*

I will set your prisoners free from the waterless pit

A waterless pit is a hopeless place of death. There is no way to satiate your thirst. It is waterless. Nothing will satisfy and there is no hope of release. But because of the blood of your covenant with God, the powerful grace of God will lift you up from any pit into which you have fallen.

> *I will extol You, O Lord, for You have lifted me up, and have not let my foes rejoice over me. O Lord my God, I cried out to You, And You healed me. O Lord, You brought my soul up from the grave; You have kept me alive, that I should not go down to the pit.*
> *~ Psalm 30:1-3*

Return to the stronghold, you prisoners of hope

The Lord is the stronghold and mighty fortress of our lives. We are weak but He is strong. Return to the stronghold and become a prisoner of hope. To be captured by the hope of God is a prison from which I never wish to be released.

*I will love You, O Lord, my strength. The Lord is my rock
and my fortress and my deliverer; My God, my strength, in
whom I will trust; My shield and the horn of my salvation,
my stronghold. I will call upon the Lord, who is worthy to be
praised; so shall I be saved from my enemies.*
~ Psalm 18:1-3

Even today I declare That I will restore double to you

The restoration of God is always double. In our limited thinking, restoration should be exactly what we lost. Not so with God. His thoughts are not our thoughts, His ways are not our ways. As the heavens are higher than the earth, so are His ways higher than our ways (see Isaiah 55:8-9). God has double restoration for you. When Job went through his great trial of faith, God restored double to him (see Job 42:10).

*Instead of your shame you shall have double honor, and
instead of confusion they shall rejoice in their portion.
Therefore in their land they shall possess double;
Everlasting joy shall be theirs.*
~ Isaiah 61:7

Dear heavenly Father,

Today I declare that I am Your prisoner of hope. I am held captive by Your love and I will never stray. I choose to believe in Your amazing restoration today. Open my eyes to the restoration You are bringing into my life. Help me to see with the eyes of faith.

In Jesus' name, Amen

Day 5

HOPE IN GOD'S WORD

*Remember the word to Your servant, upon which
You have caused me to hope. This is my comfort in my
affliction, For Your word has given me life.*
~ Psalm 119:49-50

God will speak to you very clearly. First and foremost, He speaks through the Bible. He also speaks to your inner spirit. When you know that God has spoken to you, you must put your trust in that prophetic word no matter what circumstances dictate. You can put your hope in His promises because it's impossible for Him to lie.

I hired an architect to help our church in a master planning project. He helped us design a new addition to our facility within a certain budget. The architect charged us far more than what I had agreed upon, and the plan exceeded our budget and loan capacity. So we were stuck with his expensive blueprints that we couldn't even use to build. When some folks saw that we couldn't go forward with the project, and that momentum for quick church growth was gone, they moved on. I felt terrible that I had led our church into this epic failure. I was having bad dreams of commercial airliners crashing. After consulting dream interpretation websites, I discovered that crashing jet airliners meant that there was a big failure in my life and that I was a little traumatized by it. I didn't need a dream interpretation website to tell me that.

I picked myself up and strengthened myself in the Lord (read 1 Samuel 30). I sought the Lord and petitioned Him about what direction in which we should go. The answer that came was consistent and clear, "Restructure the building you have." The church came into agreement on new plans to knock out some inner walls which nearly doubled our seating capacity. The whole project cost only about one tenth of the previously proposed new addition, and we now have almost the same seating capacity. Wow! Praise God!

The moral of the story? If what you put your hopes in crashes to the ground, look to the God of hope and He will give you a word. For every problem there is a solution.

> *Wait on the Lord; Be of good courage, and He shall strengthen your heart; Wait, I say, on the Lord!*
> *~ Psalm 27:14*

You can always put your hope in God's word for several reasons:

1. God's promises will never fail. When you put your trust and hope in God's word, you will never fail. God cannot fail. Love never fails (see 1 Corinthians 13:7-8). When you are in agreement with God's truth, you cannot fail.

> *Behold, this day I am going the way of all the earth. And you know in all your hearts and in all your souls that not one thing has failed of all the good things which the Lord your God spoke concerning you.* ***All have come to pass for you; not one word of them has failed.***
> *~ Joshua 23:14*

2. God will never lie. God's promises and His truth bring hope. Lies discourage. To walk out of hopelessness, we must cast down lying thoughts and replace them with God's truth.

> *In hope of eternal life* ***which God, who cannot lie,*** *promised before time began.*
> *~ Titus 1:2*

3. God's promises will light your path. Follow His lighted path. As you fill your mind with the hopeful promises of God, lies that bring dark hopelessness will vanish like fog in sunshine.

Your word is a lamp to my feet and a light to my path.
~ Psalm 119:105

Putting your faith in God and His word is more than just positive thinking. Positive thinking without God is dependent on you and your own strength of will. Your faith is not in you! Your faith is not in your faith or your mind power. Your faith is in the Living God who loves you and wants the best for you. Your faith is in the power of God to back up His promises and establish them in your life. God's Word is more than just mind power, it's spiritual power. It transforms your spiritual core. It infuses your inner man with strength. The Word of God will blaze the warm light of fresh hope in you. The incorruptible seed of God's Word will grow mightily and prevail over lies and hopelessness.

And you shall know the truth, and the truth shall make you free.
~ John 8:32

Let's pray this together:

Dear heavenly Father,

I pray for God-encounters today! I pray that You make Your promises personal to me. I pray that the Holy Spirit speaks to me, and brings a witness to me when I read my Bible. Make Your promises stand out so I can see how to apply them to my life and situation. Meet me when I read Your Word Lord. Show me the truth. Expose lies that I have been believing. Set me free with Your truth.

In Jesus' mighty name, Amen

Day 6

THERE IS HOPE IN YOUR FUTURE

Thus says the Lord: "Refrain your voice from weeping, And your eyes from tears; For your work shall be rewarded, says the Lord, and they shall come back from the land of the enemy. **There is hope in your future**, *says the Lord, that your children shall come back to their own border."*
~ Jeremiah 31:16-17

We hold a prayer meeting in our church every Thursday evening. They often become very intense. During every prayer meeting, God speaks to us prophetically, and the Holy Spirit witnesses to our spirits regarding things to pray about. One particular Thursday evening we felt strongly to pray for wayward children who have strayed from their faith. Grieving for spiritually lost children can be a very difficult season for any parent. As we prayed, God revealed the above Bible verses to us, and they became a prophetic promise to use in praying for unsaved children.

Praying a promise of God is a way to do spiritual warfare and bolster your faith. The promises of God give hope and light in a hopeless world, especially those applied by the Holy Spirit directly to your situation. You wage war with the sword of the Spirit, which is the Word of God (see Ephesians 6:17). You must parry, thrust and slash until they have to peel the sword from your hand. Sometimes you must become frozen to the fight. Never give up!

> *This charge I commit to you, son Timothy, according to the prophecies previously made concerning you, that by them you may wage the good warfare.*
> *~ I Timothy 1:18 NKJV*

1. Refrain your voice from weeping, and your eyes from tears for your work shall be rewarded.

> *But without faith it is impossible to please Him, for he who comes to God must believe that He is, and that He is a rewarder of those who diligently seek Him.*
> *~ Hebrews 11:6*

God is a rewarder, and He will reward your faithfulness. This is one of the reasons to refrain from weeping; He is bringing a reward your way. One huge reward is to see all your children saved and serving God. Look to the reward by keeping your faith strong.

> *But you, be strong and do not let your hands be weak,*
> **for your work shall be rewarded!**
> *~ II Chronicles 15:7*

2. Your children shall come back from the land of the enemy to their own border.

> *Therefore know that the Lord your God, He is God, the faithful God who keeps covenant and mercy for a thousand generations with those who love Him and keep His commandments.*
> *~ Deuteronomy 7:9*

I have heard several Bible teachings about generational curses, but not many about generational blessings. Because you have chosen to serve God, He has a covenant with you for a thousand generations. Your descendants have inherited a generational blessing. God will never give up on you or your offspring. His blessings are for your children, and their children and their children. Great is the reward and inheritance for those who serve the King of Kings.

> *But the mercy of the Lord is from everlasting to everlasting on those who fear Him, And His righteousness to children's children.*
> *~ Psalm 103:17*

3. There is hope in your future.

God's truth brings hope. The promises of God bring hope where there is no hope. Lies will make you hopeless. If you are battling lies, determine what lies you are believing, and then come against them in prayer.

Pray this prayer with me and let's build a foundation of hope so that we can access supernatural joy.

Dear heavenly Father,

Please expose hopeless lies. Show me where my thinking is wrong. Reveal great and precious promises to me that fill my heart with truth, light, and authentic hope. Thank You for generational blessings on me and my household. Thank You for delivering my children from the land of the enemy.

In Jesus' name, Amen

Day 7

Your Future Looks Good

For I know the thoughts that I think toward you, says the Lord, thoughts of peace and not of evil, to give you a future and a hope. Then you will call upon Me and go and pray to Me, and I will listen to you. And you will seek Me and find Me, when you search for Me with all your heart.
~ Jeremiah 29:11-13

In the early 1980's, I was a member of a Christian rock band. We traveled and played at various coffee houses, Jesus festivals, and Youth Rallies, just to name a few of the venues. Kids often asked us for our autographs, and we would debate on the bus ride home if it was appropriate to give them. We were a Christian band and wanted to give God the glory. We were evangelistic and always shared the Gospel and testimonies during our concerts. I decided that I would only give my autograph under one condition; I would also give a Bible verse with my signature. I figured that if I just left them with my signature it wouldn't leave them with much, but if I left them with an encouragement from God's Word it would carry them through life. My favorite verses to give with my name were Jeremiah 29:11-13.

These verses declare that God is not thinking bad things about you; His thoughts toward you are peace and not evil. God wants to give you a great future and a new hope. The New International Bible version quotes verse 11 this way, "For I know the plans I have for you, declares the Lord, plans to prosper you and not to harm you, plans to give you hope and a future" (Jeremiah 29:11).

God has a profound plan for your life. He plans to prosper you and give you a new hope. Your future looks good because God has things for you to do. God does not hate you. He is thinking good thoughts toward you. He may not be in agreement with some things in your life, but never doubt that He loves you and wants the best for you.

God has wonderful plans and purposes for every person. As you seek God and grow in your understanding of His Word, you will come to know more of His plan. You have been created for good works and a purpose.

> *For we are His workmanship, created in Christ Jesus*
> *for good works, which God prepared beforehand*
> *that we should walk in them.*
> *~ Ephesians 2:10*

As you move forward and obey what you know is the will of God, more light will be given you. I knew a High School student who was given a 'free ride' to a prominent college. She didn't know what to study, but a great opportunity and an open door was revealed to her. She was confused because she felt that God wanted her to go to this school but she didn't know what her career path should be. Sitting in church one Sunday morning, as I walked past her, a Bible verse popped into my mind, and I knew I was to give her this verse:

> *But the path of the just is like the shining sun, that*
> *shines ever brighter unto the perfect day.*
> *~ Proverbs 4:18*

After quoting this verse, I told her that God was lighting her path. As she obeyed God and just went forward in what she knew to do, God would give her more direction. She stared up at me for 5 seconds and then tears welled up in her eyes. This was the answer she was seeking.

God wants you to obey in the little things and He will give you more understanding and direction. Don't despise the days of small beginnings. Keep seeking. Keep being faithful with what you know to do.

Say this prayer with me.

I thank You Heavenly Father that You have a future and hope for me. I thank You that You have plans and a purpose for my life. Give me fresh hope today. I command discouragement about dreams unfulfilled to go from me now. I choose to believe that You have a better plan then what I can even imagine. I choose to walk by faith and to be faithful.
In Jesus' name, Amen

Supernatural Joy

You will show me the path of life; In Your presence is fullness of joy; At Your right hand are pleasures forevermore.
~ Psalm 16:11

Day 8

THE OIL OF JOY

*The Spirit of the Lord God is upon Me, because the Lord has anointed Me to preach good tidings to the poor; He has sent Me to heal the brokenhearted, to proclaim liberty to the captives, and the opening of the prison to those who are bound; to proclaim the acceptable year of the Lord, and the day of vengeance of our God; to comfort all who mourn, to console those who mourn in Zion, to give them beauty for ashes, **the oil of joy for mourning**, the garment of praise for the spirit of heaviness; that they may be called trees of righteousness, the planting of the Lord, that He may be glorified.*
~ Isaiah 61:1-3

A Pastor friend was about to go into a meeting that he was not looking forward to. He was meeting with an unhappy church member along with a board member who would be there as a witness and support. The church member was very upset about many things that he felt were not going his way. The Pastor did not see much chance of reconciliation on the horizon, and he thought this may end badly with the church member and his family leaving the church.

As the three of them sat down in a private office to begin to hash out their differences, they opened the meeting with prayer. Before the prayer was even over, an anointing for joy dropped into the room. The invisible oil of joy was being poured out on them. It started with snickers and then graduated to full-blown belly laughs. After ten minutes of guffawing and back-slapping humor, they forgave one another and their differences were swept away with a river of joy.

Wouldn't it be great if holy laughter fell in every meeting like that? What was even more ironic about this experience is that at that time the Pastor did not even believe that holy laughter falling was a legitimate scriptural experience (insert laughter here).

There is an anointing for joy; a supernatural endowment from the Spirit of God to overcome all mourning, despondency, and sorrow, and then experience supernatural joy. Jesus was the "anointed" one. That's what "Messiah" in the Hebrew language, and "Christ" in the Greek language means; Jesus is THE anointed one. The above scripture is a messianic prophecy. This is the mission statement of the Messiah. He came to deliver us from the brokenness caused by sin and the devil. He came to give beauty for ashes, and joy for mourning. This powerful anointing that was on Jesus has now been given to the body of Christ. This mission statement now belongs to the church, the body of Christ in THIS world. Jesus ascended into heaven and sent the Holy Spirit to empower the church to continue His mission. If there was ever a time that the church needs joy and holy laughter it would be now. The supernatural joy of the Lord is our strength to do the work of ministry (see Nehemiah 8:10).

In the Old Testament times, when someone was called and commissioned into the offices of a priest, king or prophet, the holy anointing oil was poured on their heads (see Psalm 133). This symbolized the grace and power of the Holy Spirit coming upon them to fulfill their call (see Exodus 30:22-33).

Then Samuel took the horn of oil and anointed him in the midst of his brothers; and the Spirit of the Lord came upon David from that day forward. So Samuel arose and went to Ramah.
~ I Samuel 16:13

When David was a young shepherd boy, the prophet Samuel poured the anointing oil upon his head. From that moment on David had a kingly anointing. He possessed the ability to be king years before he sat on the throne. He became a king on the inside before he became a king outwardly. Every believer in Christ now possesses an anointing to rule. You and I have a greater anointing available than that which was available to the Old Testament saints.

> *To Him who loved us and washed us from our sins in His own blood, and has made us kings and priests to His God and Father, to Him be glory and dominion forever and ever. Amen.*
> *~ Revelation 1:5b-6*

> *But now He has obtained a more excellent ministry, inasmuch as He is also Mediator of **a better covenant, which was established on better promises.***
> *~ Hebrews 8:6*

When you were born again and indwelt by the Holy Spirit, you received this anointing. You just need to learn how to access it by faith. You can have what the Word of God says that you can have. You are what the Word of God says that you are. That is what this book is all about. It's about learning of the joy that is ours in Christ, accessing it by faith, and living in victory.

> *Love has been perfected among us in this: that we may have boldness in the day of judgment; **because as He is, so are we in this world.***
> *~ I John 4:17*

Think about that; as Jesus is, so are WE in this world! The same anointing of joy and gladness that was on Jesus is on you and me! It's time to claim your inheritance. It's time to confess what Jesus has purchased for you with His precious blood.

> *You have loved righteousness and hated lawlessness; Therefore God, **Your God, has anointed You With the oil of gladness** more than Your companions.*
> *~ Hebrews 1:9*

Supernatural Joy

Prayer:

Dear Father in heaven, fill me with Your supernatural joy today. Help me to learn how to access Your joy by faith. Help me to learn strategies to maintain my joy. I thank You for this anointing. Thank You for Your provision of joy and laughter.

In Jesus' name, Amen.

Declaration:

I receive God's free gift of salvation. I thank You God that Your free gift of salvation includes the oil of gladness. No longer will I allow any demonic oppression to rob me of my inheritance of joy and healing. I declare today that I will learn how to walk in God's supernatural joy and reject thoughts of hopelessness and despondency.

Day 9

God's Favor Brings Joy

But let all those rejoice who put their trust in You; Let them ever shout for joy, because You defend them; Let those also who love Your name be joyful in You. For You, O Lord will bless the righteous; With favor You will surround him as with a shield.
~ Psalm 5:11-12

What a heritage you and I have as Christians! God promises to bless you, defend you, and surround you with a wall of favor. All great reasons to shore up your mind with fresh hope. Declare God's favor over yourself every day. God's favor will bring confidence, promotion, and wonderful opportunities to minister to others. Rejoice! Shout for joy! Let those who love His name be joyful in Him!

I was newly married and needed to make more money. I heard that a friend had started a small business and needed a salesman. I was confident that I could be a great salesman because I could talk to almost anyone. I went to his house and told him that if he trained me, I would go to offices and industrial parks and sell his products. He taught me what I needed to know and we put together a book that I could flip through and give presentations. His company had made only a total of $40K gross sales that past year, so he couldn't make any promises as to my success. We agreed on a commission and I hit the road.

As I went out cold calling (a sales term for personally visiting a business without an appointment), I would confess Psalm 5:12, *"Thank You Oh God that You have surrounded me with favor as with a shield. Let Your supernatural favor be seen on me today. Open up doors of blessing. If You see that a business will not be a good blessing, close the door to that customer. In Jesus' name, Amen."*

When I introduced myself at potential customers' front desks and handed them my business card, I was immediately ushered into the office of a CEO, manager, or decision-maker. My presentation was always the same. I used no gimmicks, pressure, or manipulation tactics. I would simply say, "I want to help you save money. It's to my advantage that I help you and give you good service because then you will keep using our products and recommend me to others. For this reason, I will do my best to make you happy." In the first year, our company's gross sales more than doubled. The next year our company's gross sales more than doubled again. I had to hire and train more salesmen, and our company bought a building to contain sales offices and product storage. In the third year, our company's gross sales more than doubled again! When the Lord finally called me to leave sales and step into full-time ministry, our company was grossing more than a million dollars a year! We sold office supplies, not big-ticket items like real estate, so that was amazing growth to increase from $40K in gross sales to over a million in just four years. I believe our success was because I prayed and declared the favor of God over my life.

God does not show favoritism. If He gave me supernatural favor, He can do it for you too. You need to believe in God's ability to surround you with supernatural favor. You are highly favored; God wants to bless you. Change the way you think. In your mind, begin to change images of rejection with images of acceptance. Hold your head up and declare what the scriptures say about you. This is not just positive thinking. You are reprograming your spirit with the truth of God's Word.

> **The Lord was with Joseph, and he was a successful man**; and he was in the house of his master the Egyptian. And his master saw that the Lord was with him and that the Lord made all he did to prosper in his hand. **So Joseph found favor in his sight**, and served him. Then he made him overseer of his house, and all that he had he put under his authority.
> ~ Genesis 39:2-4

The above scripture is an example of what divine favor can do. You have divine favor because God is with you, just like Joseph. God can make everything you do prosper. Expansion of influence, promotion, and greater responsibility is the result of claiming God's favor on your life. It's not prideful to claim what God has already given you. God loves you and wants you to advance. Your success and advancement will bring God glory. You pining away in self-pity, negative thinking and low self-esteem does no one any good. You can have what the Word of God says that you can have. You are what the Word of God says that you are. If you are trying your best to obey what you know is the will of God for your life, then you can claim the favor of God.

Prayer declaration:

Thank You Oh God that you have surrounded me with favor as with a shield according to Psalm 5:12. Let Your supernatural favor be seen on me today. Open up doors of blessing. I determine to be joyful and rejoice in Your divine protection and favor.

In Jesus' name, Amen

Day 10

Joy is Found in Giving

So let each one give as he purposes in his heart, not grudgingly or of necessity; for God loves a cheerful giver.
~ II Corinthians 9:7

The word cheerful is the Greek word "hilaros" from which we get our English word "hilarious". There can be such enjoyment in giving that it sweeps away all restraints. Supernatural joy can be accessed by being a giver of gifts. One of the most quoted New Testament verses relating to giving is John 3:16.

For God so loved the world that He gave His only begotten Son, that whoever believes in Him should not perish but have everlasting life.
~ John 3:16

God's love caused Him to give. God is not a cheap giver; He gave the best He had to give. He gave His ONLY Son, the most precious thing He possessed. Love gives, and love accesses great joy from giving with no strings attached. Freely we have received, and freely we should give. God will reward us; we shouldn't look to man for our reward. You can't out-give God; we give and God rewards. We give out of love for God and His people, and yet God loves to reward wholesome giving. It's an endless cycle of love expressed through giving.

One time I gave a gift to a ministry on Christmas Eve, and just after I gave it, a belly laugh came over me that lasted

Supernatural Joy

2 or 3 minutes. I could have tried to restrain it, but I just gave myself over to it. The laughter was coming from my spirit as a supernatural joy came upon me. Be filled with the joy of the Lord. There is healing in God's supernatural joy. Don't despair; instead, give and let God's joy overtake all sorrow.

Secret-giving also releases supernatural joy. During a home prayer meeting, a woman had a vision of empty cupboards, so we took a monetary collection, and then a friend and I were elected to buy some groceries. We took the grocery 'care package' to the home of someone I knew had been laid off from work, and their young family was in need. However, the father refused the groceries because of pride. I was discouraged and called my Pastor who prayed with me over the phone. He assured me that I had heard from God and I should still listen to Him (see John 10:27).

I received new directions from the Holy Spirit and knew what I had to do. During the song service at our church on Sunday morning, my friend and I slipped out to the parking lot and loaded the groceries into a car. The next Sunday, the couple who owned the car stood up to give testimony about how they had empty cupboards and an angel put groceries into their car while they were at church the week before. I turned to my friend and said, "You're not my idea of a handsome angel." His response was," Speak for yourself." We had such a good laugh.

Generosity is a contact point to receive supernatural joy.

> *Restore to me the joy of Your salvation, and*
> *uphold me by Your generous Spirit.*
> *~ Psalm 51:12*

Dear Heavenly Father, help me to have a generous spirit. Teach me to be a giver. Lead me in the adventure and joy of being a hilarious giver.
In Jesus' name, Amen

Day 11

There is Joy in God's Presence

*You will show me the path of life; In **Your presence is fullness of joy**; At Your right hand are pleasures forevermore.*
~ Psalm 16:11

For You have made him most blessed forever; You have made him exceedingly glad with Your presence.
~ Psalm 21:6

Although my wife and I had three beautiful daughters, we both felt that our family was not yet complete. We wanted another baby. My wife, at that time, was 43 years old and many advised against it. While she was pregnant, we had to sit and listen to the doctor rattle off all the complications and dangers of having a baby at age 43. The doctor was just doing his job, but Nicole was very upset. I assured her that we had heard from God to have another baby, and everything was going to go great. Some of our friends even told us we were crazy for having a child so late in life. After all, we were just about to enjoy our freedom from raising children, so why have another one? It wouldn't have done any good trying to convince them that we had heard from God on this, so we just shrugged it off as "well-meaning friends." I told Nicole, "What else are we going to do? We might as well raise another one."

Supernatural Joy

After fathering three girls, I was hoping for a boy. We had even agreed on a boy's name; Noah Gates. Through the ultrasound, we discovered the baby was a girl. I really wasn't disappointed because I trust in God's sovereignty in such matters. As Nicole was reading the Gospel of Luke one morning, she came across this verse: And the angel answered and said to him, "I am Gabriel, who stands in the presence of God, and was sent to speak to you and bring you these glad tidings." Luke 1:19

Gabriel stood in the presence of God! In God's presence is fullness of Joy! From the presence of God comes words of glad tidings! Nicole and I knew from this verse that our baby girl's name would be Gabriella and her middle name would be Joy. As it turned out, Gabby's name was very prophetic. Not only has she been a source of great joy to our lives, but she is a walking prophetic word as God brings great joy to the body of Christ through Gabby's life. His presence will become greater and greater in these last days. Although there is great darkness in the world, the glory of the Lord will arise in the church (see Isaiah 60:1-2)!

Theologically, we all know that our God is omnipresent, or universally present. But there is a difference between God being universally present and His manifest presence. God manifested Himself to Moses on the backside of a desert through a burning bush. Jesus was teaching on a certain day, and the manifest presence of God showed up and brought healing virtue. The Bible depicts the difference between God's omnipresence and His manifest presence.

> *Now it happened on a certain day, as He was teaching, that there were Pharisees and teachers of the law sitting by, who had come out of every town of Galilee, Judea, and Jerusalem.*
> ***And the power of the Lord was present to heal them.***
> *~ Luke 5:17*

You and I need the manifest presence of God. In His presence is fulness of joy. How do we experience His presence? Where do we go to find it? I will tell you the tried and true method; He manifests Himself in worship. Not just any worship; wholehearted passionate worship. When there is a full abandonment in worship, a consecration, and a complete dedication of our lives, He WILL show up. Joy and words of glad tidings follow.

You can enter into worship alone and experience some amazing God encounters. Do this: when you are alone, lift your hands high (over your head, no half-mast stuff) and begin to praise the Lord. Tell Him how awesome He is; that type of worship is called magnifying the Lord. Make Him bigger than the problems. You can't out-give God. You give Him your praise and He will shower you with His joyful presence.

The next thing to do is go to church. Get into corporate worship. Folks who are struggling with depression generally want to stay away from people. However, if you are going to overcome, you have to resist isolation. You need God and God's people. Look at this verse: For where two or three are gathered together in My name, I am there in the midst of them. Matthew 18:20

Please say this declaration prayer:

Dear God,

Thank You so much for Your presence. I determine to worship You until I sense Your glory. Let me experience Your joyful presence today. I will magnify You and make You bigger than my problems. Show me Your glory.

In Jesus' name, Amen

Day 12

Ask, That Your Joy May Be Full

*Until now you have asked nothing in My name. Ask, and you will receive, **that your joy may be full**.*
~ John 16:24

And these things we write to you that your joy may be full.
~ I John 1:4

*These things I have spoken to you, that My joy may remain in you, and **that your joy may be full**.*
~ John 15:11

These Bible verses make it completely clear that God wants you to be full of joy. Are you full of Joy? Now is the time to ask, so that your joy may be full. What is hindering your joy from being full?

One day as I walked by our church bookkeeper's desk, I heard him mumble, "Oh this will never happen" as he threw some papers into the trash can. I asked him what he had tossed away. It was a magazine advertisement to go on a trip to the Holy Land, Israel. He and his wife had always wanted to go there, but they believed there was no way they could ever afford it.

Supernatural Joy

At this point, I pulled the magazine ad out of the trash and asked him if he really wanted to go. He responded by repeating his financial plight and confessed poverty and lack. My response was, "Jesus said, 'Ask, and you will receive, that your joy may be full.'" What will it hurt if we just ask the Lord for the money?" We laid our hands on the magazine article and came into agreement in prayer.

Again I say to you that if two of you agree on earth concerning anything that they ask, it will be done for them by My Father in heaven.
~ Matthew 18:19

Some folks in the church caught wind of the bookkeeper and his wife's desire to go to the Holy Land, and they started taking a secret collection for their cause. They then gave the money to the couple, but it still wasn't quite enough for the trip. Then a lumber company made a generous offer to the bookkeeper to select-cut some of the trees on his property. That resulted in the couple having more than enough to enjoy a first-class, guided tour of the Holy Land.

What is stealing your joy? Ask, and you shall receive that your joy may be full.

Make a short list of the things that are robbing you of your joy. Pray about them. Talk to a friend who is full of faith about some of these issues. Agree together in prayer and watch God move mountains to fill you with His joy. After all, what does it hurt to ask?

Day 13

God Rejoices Over You

*The Lord your God in your midst, The Mighty One, will save; He will rejoice over you with gladness, He will quiet you with His love, **He will rejoice** over you with singing.*
~ Zephaniah 3:17

The word "rejoice," is the Hebrew word "gil" (Strong's #1523), meaning joy, rejoice, and be glad. To leap and dance for joy. To spin around with intense motion. This word for rejoice lays to rest the notion that joy is just an inner sense of wellbeing. God is so happy and joyful that He is DANCING and singing over His people. Despite what some people may believe, God is not always in a perpetual state of anger; He is also the source of intense joy!

During the worship service at a Youth Conference, my wife Nicole had a vision. Jesus rose from His throne and started dancing wildly over the young people at the conference. He was leaping and spinning in ecstatic joy. His dance was also warlike. It was a form of intercession over the next generation. Two things were new to me about this vision: the first was that Jesus danced, and danced wildly with abandonment, and the second was that I had never thought of a "dance" being a form of intercession. It makes sense that dancing can be intercession. Native Americans performed prayer dances. Dancing is a form of communication, so why not communicate to God with movement? God is so full of joy over you; He celebrates you with a dance of joy. The joy of the Lord is infectious; He imparts joy and makes joyful those He celebrates.

> *Also that day they offered great sacrifices, and rejoiced,*
> **for God had made them rejoice with great joy;**
> *the women and the children also rejoiced, so*
> *that the joy of Jerusalem was heard afar off.*
> *~ Nehemiah 12:43*

> *Then he said to them, "Go your way, eat the fat, drink the sweet, and send portions to those for whom nothing is prepared; for this day is holy to our Lord. Do not sorrow,*
> **for the joy of the Lord is your strength."**
> *~ Nehemiah 8:10*

We have the privilege of experiencing God's joy. It is an expressive joy; a joy that can give uncommon strength. The Joy of the Lord can transform atmospheres and lift the spirit of heaviness.

I was on staff as a Youth Pastor when our church called a special prayer meeting. Our church needed a spiritual breakthrough. We needed to be more "on fire." We had slumped into a dry and apathetic place. (At least we recognized our need, some churches keep hobbling on in that dry state until they blindly stumble over a cliff into oblivion.) At least 25 people attended to press in for a measure of revival. The lights in the sanctuary were turned down low and the dirge music was pensive. At first I thought we were at a funeral service rather than at a prayer meeting for fervent revival. Maybe we should just lay the church to rest in a shallow grave and all move on with our lives?

The music eventually kicked up a bit and eventually became almost warlike. I was in front of everyone, facing the cross on the podium when God's still small voice spoke to me, "Will you dance for me?" I immediately began testing the spirits to see if this was God. Why would God ask me to dance for Him? I'm not a dancer, and I thought I would look like a complete idiot and make a fool of myself if I started dancing at this dead prayer meeting. I thought it might be easier to dance at a big hipster worship service where all the young people were in the front jumping up and down, but not here. The Lord heard the conflict going on in my heart and repeated the question, "Would you dance for ME?" The emphasis was a little more on the "ME" this time. It was as though God was asking if I loved Him enough to make a fool of myself. Well, I decided I did love God enough to dance for Him, so I started dancing.

As I stepped out in faith and started dancing, the Spirit of God came over me and I began doing a warlike, native American dance. It was very fervent, like I was interceding through the dance. I must have jumped, bounced, and gyrated like that for five to ten minutes until I was very sweaty and out of breath. Then the Spirit of God spoke to me and told me to turn around and look behind me. As I began to turn around, I expected everyone to be staring at the Youth Pastor who was having a nervous breakdown in living color right in front of them. Instead, everyone was leaping and dancing. It was wild pandemonium. Everyone was caught up in the fervor of the Spirit. The heavens were open and vitality was once again being poured out onto our church.

Afterward, folks were asking me how I could dance like that? It was awesome! There was such a glory coming off of me as I made war with the dance; I had entered into the joy and strength of the Lord. To this day I have never again danced like that.

God wants you to transform the spiritual atmosphere around you. From a smothering death to a living vitality, from confusion to clarity, from despondency to joy, from darkness to light, from oppression to freedom. Let's lay hold of the Joy of the Lord today.

Dear Heavenly Father,

I take authority over the atmosphere around me. I command joy to fill my spirit now! Let me be a partaker of Your Joy Father. Fill me now.

In Jesus' name, Amen

Now begin to worship the Lord! Lift your hands and tell God how much you love Him and how great He is. Give thanks and say, "You are good, and Your mercy endures forever!"

These things I have spoken to you, that My joy may remain in you, and that your joy may be full.
~ John 15:11

Day 14

Joy Comes in the Morning

For His anger is but for a moment, His favor is for life;
Weeping may endure for a night,
but joy comes in the morning.
~ Psalm 30:5

The truth I want to convey here is that weeping and pain are transitory. One minute things can appear completely hopeless and then suddenly...everything changes. I like the book of Proverbs, but I don't always like platitudes. The one that comes to mind is, "This too shall pass." The reason I don't like these clichés is that when I'm in the middle of a trial in my life and someone says, "This too shall pass," I'm tempted to belt them in their insensitive face.

I think you get my point that things can change suddenly. Weeping may endure for a night, but joy comes in the morning. Three times in the book of Acts things changed suddenly.

> *And suddenly there came a sound from heaven, as of a rushing mighty wind, and it filled the whole house where they were sitting. When the Day of Pentecost had fully come, they were all with one accord in one place.*
> *~ Acts 2:1-2*

The disciples were in the upper room praying and suddenly they were transformed by the power of the Holy Spirit and became courageous witnesses.

Supernatural Joy

> *But at midnight Paul and Silas were praying and singing hymns to God, and the prisoners were listening to them. Suddenly there was a great earthquake, so that the foundations of the prison were shaken; and immediately all the doors were opened and everyone's chains were loosed.*
> *~ Acts 16:25-26*

Paul and Silas were in prison and suddenly everything changed. They were not only set free, but all the prisoners were set free and the jailer and his family received Christ!

> *Now it happened, as I journeyed and came near Damascus at about noon, suddenly a great light from heaven shone around me.*
> *~ Acts 22:6*

One minute Paul was hunting down Christians, then suddenly he was transformed by a visitation from Jesus! Talk about your 180 degrees turn around. I think you get my point; God can turn hopeless situations around. Just be patient and wait on Him.

> *For our light affliction, which is but for a moment, is working for us a far more exceeding and eternal weight of glory, while we do not look at the things which are seen, but at the things which are not seen. For the things which are seen are temporary, but the things which are not seen are eternal.*
> *~ II Corinthians 4:17-18*

Everything that is seen is temporary and subject to change. You have to learn to see beyond the temporary; you must see through the eyes of faith. Through faith, things can change suddenly, or they can change slowly. Some things have to change because when the temporary comes up against the eternal, and the movable comes up against the immovable, the temporary has to change. When you take the eternal Word of God to a temporal problem, your problem has to change. The Word of God is not going to change. Hallelujah!

Supernatural Joy

*For in the time of trouble He shall hide me in His pavilion;
In the secret place of His tabernacle He shall hide me;
He shall set me high upon a rock. And now my head
shall be lifted up above my enemies all around me;
Therefore I will offer sacrifices of joy in His tabernacle;
I will sing, yes, I will sing praises to the Lord.
~ Psalm 27:5-6*

Prayer declaration:

Thank You, Lord God, that there is always hope with you. I can call upon You in time of trouble and You have promised to help me. I WILL offer sacrifices of joy in Your tabernacle. Weeping is only temporary. Joy comes in the morning. I live in expectation of seeing joy on the other side of pain.

In Jesus' name, Amen

HOLY LAUGHTER

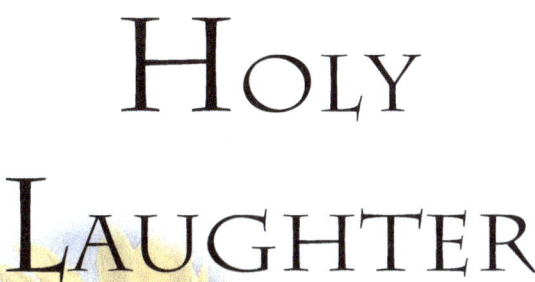

Don't ever waste an opportunity to have a good belly laugh.
~Alan Leonhardt

Day 15

HE CAUSES LAUGHTER

Now Abraham was one hundred years old when his son Isaac was born to him. And Sarah said, "God has made me laugh, and all who hear will laugh with me." She also said, "Who would have said to Abraham that Sarah would nurse children? For I have borne him a son in his old age."
~ Genesis 21:5-7

Although I had experienced supernatural joy and Holy laughter, the church I was pastoring had not. Many were skeptical of things that they had not experienced personally. I asked one of my favorite preachers, Dr. Leon van Rooyen (Global Ministries and Relief Inc), to visit our church in the woods of Northern Lower Michigan and speak at a series of meetings. I don't like to dictate what subject matter on which the guest speaker will speak. I would rather that they listen to the Holy Spirit's prompting; the Spirit knows what we need.

Before the first evening meeting, I asked the Doc what he felt led to speak on. He told me that the church needs joy and laughter. I had been praying that our church would receive an infusion of Holy laughter, but when it was about to be poured out, I became insecure. Would the church receive the supernatural outpouring of joy, or would they reject it as weird? I have learned that when the Doc receives a word from the Holy Spirit you don't question it; I had no choice but to trust God.

That evening Dr. van Rooyen began sharing that when he first heard about Holy laughter, he did not receive it. He was pastoring a substantial church in South Africa at the time and they were somewhat reserved and conservative. The Holy Spirit challenged him to study the scriptures on the subject and the Doc was overwhelmed by many verses that he previously overlooked. That evening he shared about the promised son Isaac, whose name means, "He will cause laughter"; this is the type of Christ who gives us victorious laughter!

As the Doc shared scripture after scripture from the Bible about laughter, a couple of people started giggling. Then a few more. Then some started outright laughing. Then, as if a cracked dam was bursting forth, the meeting erupted in outrageous laughter. Chains of despondency, grieving and depression were broken as supernatural joy filled the sanctuary. Praise the Lord!

God wants to fill you with laughter, and the joy of the Lord will spill over into the lives of those around you. All who hear will laugh with you.

Thank you, Heavenly Father.
I receive your joy and laughter now in the name of your Holy child, Jesus.

Pray the above prayer out loud and begin laughing by faith. Be a fool for Christ. It may start as a giggle, and then a chuckle, and then a belly laugh. Access the joy of the Lord now. Don't be afraid. Just do it!

Therefore I say to you, whatever things you ask when you pray, believe that you receive them, and you will have them.
~ Mark 11:24

Day 16

HE WILL FILL YOUR MOUTH WITH LAUGHING

*He will yet fill your mouth with laughing,
And your lips with rejoicing.
~ Job 8:21*

Why is it that some of us have so much trouble with the concept of Holy laughter? It's God that wants to make you laugh. When people are under contrition for their sins and weep in repentance, we have no problem understanding that emotion. If God can cause a sorrow for sin that cleanses the heart, can't He also cause a joy that erupts in contagious laughter? Yes! That is what His Word says, "He will fill your mouth with laughter."

I was 21 when a friend and I fully committed our lives to Christ. We were convinced that we should be baptized since we had become true believers. We had both been baptized as babies in a traditional church but were now convinced by scripture that baptism follows a heartfelt profession of faith in Christ.

Now as they went down the road, they came to some water. And the eunuch said, "See, here is water. What hinders me from being baptized?" Then Philip said, "If you believe with all your heart, you may." And he answered and said, "I believe

Holy Laughter

that Jesus Christ is the Son of God."
~ Acts 8:36-37

During one Sunday evening service at our church, we both took the plunge. This was not a little sprinkle on our heads, this was a baptismal tank. The pastor dunked us fully under the tepid water. The Pastor jokingly warned me that he may have to hold me under the water longer than the others.

Everyone who was baptized that evening wore white robes and gave a short testimony while waste deep in the tank. Some of us resembled wet rats when we exited the tank in front of a couple hundred people. We didn't care about what we looked like; we were so full of joy in our new-found freedom in Christ.

As I was driving to our homes that evening, we rode along in a comfortable silence, happy that we obeyed God. I asked my friend how he felt when he came up out of the water. He said in a dry tone, "I felt wet." We glanced at each other for two seconds and then busted out laughing. The joy of the Lord hit us so hard that I began driving a little erratically. I pulled over to the side of the highway, we got out of the car and bent over laughing for another five or ten minutes.

This was my first experience with Holy laughter. Sure, I could have quenched it, but why would I do that? Why does anyone want to suppress such supernatural joy? Don't ever waste an opportunity to have a good belly laugh.

Dear Father in Heaven,
  Help me never to suppress Your joy. Your joy is a gift to me. I will give myself over to Your healing joy. Let Your joy wash over me and cleanse me from all defeat and despondency.
  In Jesus' name, Amen

Day 17

LAUGHING IS INTERCESSION

He who sits in the heavens shall laugh; The Lord shall hold them in derision. Then He shall speak to them in His wrath, And distress them in His deep displeasure.
~ Psalm 2:4-5

But You, O Lord, shall laugh at them; You shall have all the nations in derision. I will wait for You, O You his Strength; For God is my defense. My God of mercy shall come to meet me; God shall let me see my desire on my enemies.
~ Psalm 59:8-10

I remember listening to a teaching by Kenneth Hagan about laughing at the devil; he declared with authority, "Ha, ha, ha, Mr. Devil. Ha, ha, ha, Mr. Devil." As I spoke the same and forced myself to laugh, I felt *my* authority rising inside me. I began to realize that laughing is a form of intercession.

Recently, I listened to another amazing Bible teacher, Steve Backlund (Igniting Hope Ministries), and he would declare, "Let's just laugh at that lie." Steve understood that laughing becomes a spiritual weapon used to take down strongholds and every thought that exalted itself against the knowledge of God (see 2 Corinthians 10:4-6).

Some years ago, when I pastored a church in Northern Lower Michigan, a man and wife left our church and went on the warpath against my ministry. It was very difficult for me because I loved these folks and felt betrayed, angry and hurt. I know that I am supposed to forgive people by faith, but it was so difficult to overcome my anger when I heard reports of the "current lie" they were spreading around the community.

My wife and I were forced to drive by their home every time we wanted to go to the local grocery store, and I couldn't resist looking in their driveway to see if any of my church members were visiting and buying into their hate. I know that seems petty, but I was not in a good state of mind at the time. Then one day everything shifted. As I drove by their home, I began to laugh. And laugh, and laugh, and laugh. At first, I thought I might be having a nervous breakdown. But then I realized it was a laughter of intercession. "Ha, Ha Mr. Devil. Let's just laugh at those lies..." I laughed until I was at peace and had faith that God was taking care of the situation. What was so huge in my head was infinitesimal to almighty God. After this laughing incident, every time I drove past their home, I would go into a belly laugh. It was a supernatural laugh; a healing laugh of intercession.

There are places of glory to which we are given access that transcend conventional Christian tradition and experience. Because I was exposed to Holy laughter and surrendered to it, laughing in the Holy Spirit became easier to access. Many times, I laugh in the Spirit when I am stressed and when I sense a victory in the spirit realm. Don't knock it until you've tried it. It's in the prideful nature of self-righteous Christians to mock, criticize and ridicule things that they haven't experienced personally. If it's okay to weep in prayer, then it's okay to laugh in prayer.

How would you like to access some Holy laughter in your life? Start saying out loud, "HA HA HA MR DEVIL! HA HA HA MR DEVIL!" Come on, you've got to loosen up a bit. Do it again and keep doing it until you are actually laughing, Bahahaha. Just start laughing at some lies, like:

- God's not going to take care of me in the future. Ha ha ha ha ha (see Philippians 4:19).
- I'm not lovable. Ha ha ha ha ha (see John 3:16).
- I will never do anything of any significance. Ha ha ha ha ha (see Psalm 92:13-15).
- I will die before my time. Ha ha ha ha ha (see Psalm 91:16).

You get the picture. Don't skip this exercise. You may have to put it off until you are in a place where folks won't think you're insane when they hear you shouting, "HA HA HA MR DEVIL." But don't skip this; I want you to be filled with a joy inexpressible and full of glory (see 1 Peter 1:8).

Day 18

LAUGHTER IS HEALING

*A merry heart does good, like medicine,
but a broken spirit dries the bones.
~ Proverbs 17:22*

A merry heart and laughter cause healing; it's like a medicine. Have you taken your medicine today? When we are laughing, powerful hormones called endorphins are released in the brain and nervous system. Endorphins are similar to morphine and are natural painkillers. Also, endorphins can bring about feelings of euphoria. In other words, laughing makes you feel great! These same endorphins are released when we do even moderate exercise. So, go take a walk while listening to a comedian YouTube video, and you will be getting a double shot of endorphins.

So, let's kickstart your endorphin production with an exercise. Track with me and humor me. The best thing is to laugh at yourself and don't take yourself so seriously. I'm not talking about a self-deprecating, mean-spirited, put-down kind of ridicule. I'm talking about having fun and laughing at your own goofiness. I don't always trust people who can't laugh at themselves.

Here's the exercise: Go to your bathroom mirror (any mirror will do, but you may need some privacy). Look at yourself and force a smile. See how goofy you look and celebrate it.

Keep smiling, don't stop. Now, start laughing at yourself. I'll wait...

Feel better? I'll bet you do.

Now, go to a friend, or family member, and tell them you want to have a little fun. Sit or stand facing each other and smile broadly. Soon you will both be smiling and start giggling, and then you will be laughing at each other. This never fails, trust me. Here is another way to kickstart your endorphins. Watch an episode of your favorite sitcom or a YouTube video of your favorite stand-up comedian. There is plenty of clean comedy available; there is currently a huge demand for Christian comedians. Some Christian comedians are filling small stadiums with their performances and they sell more tickets than big rock bands. Laughing is fun and most of all, healthy.

A time to weep, and a time to laugh;
A time to mourn, and a time to dance.
~ Ecclesiastes 3:4

Rejoice with those who rejoice, and
weep with those who weep.
~ Romans 12:15

There is a time to mourn and weep, and to express real hurt. But we must also heal and overcome. After a time of weeping, God has given us the gift of laughter to help us heal. Take your medicine today. God is teaching you how to access His supernatural joy.

Sing praise to the Lord, you saints of His, and give thanks at
the remembrance of His holy name. For His anger is but for
a moment, His favor is for life; Weeping may endure for a
night, but joy comes in the morning.
~ Psalm 30:4-5

Day 19

LAUGHTER IS VICTORY

When the Lord brought back the captivity of Zion, we were like those who dream. Then our mouth was filled with laughter, And our tongue with singing. Then they said among the nations, "The Lord has done great things for them." The Lord has done great things for us, and we are glad.
~ Psalm 126:1-3

Here we have laughter filling our mouths as a result of deliverance and victory. There are times during prayer meetings that I spontaneously laugh. Sometimes people look at me with a weird look that asks, "What's so funny?" It's just that I sense a victory in the spirit and it causes me great joy. It is more than an inner feeling of contentment; it's a belly laugh. It's a rip-roaring knee slapper.

In the late 1990s, I attended some renewal meetings during a conference at the Airport Church in Toronto, Canada. At the end of two meetings, I stood in the prayer line and waited for a prayer team to pray with me. A team of three finally approached me, and the woman leading the group was very sweet and gentle. As they prayed, "More Lord, more Lord," I began to weep a heartfelt cry of repentance. After the lament, I sensed a great victory and laughed loudly and for a long time.

The same pattern happened both times I received prayer that day. First, I would weep, then I would sense a victory, then

Supernatural Joy

I would laugh. I didn't know quite what to think about it so I just put in on the back burner of my mind and shrugged it off. During the drive home from the conference, a friend asked me if I received anything? I wasn't sure what kind of impartation I had received.

The next Sunday morning at church, the Pastor asked if I would pray for all the young people between the ages of 12 and 18. They came forward and made a prayer line. My wife, Nicole, and I began to lay hands on them individually. At first, they all began to weep, then they sensed a victory and many laughed. Three of them laughed for the rest of the service! I kid you not.

Ever since that conference at the Toronto Airport Church, I laugh when I sense victory. I discovered that it's okay to outwardly, and unashamedly, express victory in the form of laughing and shouting. Don't hold back. Laughing is so good for you. You don't have to see the victory with your physical eyes; you see it with your spiritual eyes. When you sense victory, laugh, laugh, laugh. God is bringing you out of captivity. He wants to fill your mouth with laughter.

In the mighty name of Jesus,
I will pray through to victory. I will not hold back my laughter. I ask You Father to unstop the well of joy inside of me. I WILL have my victory laugh. I WILL have the last laugh. Thank you, God, for filling my mouth with supernatural laughter.
Amen

Therefore with joy you will draw water
From the wells of salvation.
~ Isaiah 12:3

Day 20

Obedience Brings Joy

"Come now, and let us reason together," Says the Lord, "Though your sins are like scarlet, they shall be as white as snow; Though they are red like crimson, they shall be as wool. If you are willing and obedient, you shall eat the good of the land."
~ Isaiah 1:18-19

There are several roots and causes of depression; trauma, anxiety, fearfulness, and hope deferred. You could rephrase "hope deferred" as "a terrible disappointment leading to hopelessness."

Anxiety in the heart of man causes depression, but a good word makes it glad.
~ Proverbs 12:2

Hope deferred makes the heart sick, but when the desire comes, it is a tree of life.
~ Proverbs 13:12

There is one cause of depression that is rarely discussed; disobedience. Yes, that's right, plain old stubborn rebellion against God's will for your life will ultimately lead to a joyless destination. You must stop justifying your rebellion and admit it to God, repent and begin to obey. "If you are willing and obedient, you shall eat the good of the land" (Isaiah 1:19). I'm not trying to put some kind of pharisaical shame on you, I'm trying to get you set free. When we live in willful disobedience to God, we walk out from His protective covering and are vulnerable to demonic oppression. We must first submit to God and then we can resist the devil. The good news is that you CAN be set free; it's never too late to get back on the right track.

> *Therefore submit to God. Resist the devil*
> *and he will flee from you.*
> *~ James 4:7*

> *You have caused men to ride over our heads; We*
> *went through fire and through water; But You*
> *brought us out to rich fulfillment.*
> *~ Psalm 66:12*

Here are two Bible verses that show how confusion and depression can sometimes have a root cause of disobedience, and un-thankfulness.

1. Because, although they knew God, they did not glorify Him as God, nor were thankful, but became futile in their thoughts, and their foolish hearts were darkened. Romans 1:21.

   This verse states that there was knowledge of God, but because of disregard for Him and not being thankful, futile thoughts overtook their minds and a darkness crept over their heart.

2. The Lord will strike you with madness and blindness and confusion of heart. And you shall grope at noonday, as a blind man gropes in darkness; you shall not prosper in your ways; you shall be only oppressed and plundered continually, and no one shall save you. Deuteronomy 28:28-29.

Deuteronomy chapter 28 lists the blessings of obedience in the first 14 verses, and then the curses of disobedience in the next 54 verses. Madness, blindness, and confusion are part of the curses of disobedience.

But it shall come to pass, if you do not obey the voice of the Lord your God, to observe carefully all His commandments and His statutes which I command you today, that all these curses will come upon you and overtake you.
Deuteronomy 28:15

Say this prayer of repentance out loud and God will begin to bring restoration and joy back to your life! "If you are willing and obedient, you shall eat the good of the land" (Isaiah 1:19).

Dear Heavenly Father,
I ask your forgiveness for my sin and disobedience. I vow to follow Your plan for my life and not my own. Please deliver me from darkness and bring fresh hope into my life. No sacrifice is too big for me to have the joy of the Lord. By Your strength, I forsake what I know is wrong. I receive your joy and restoration now, In Jesus mighty name,
Amen.

Day 21

Praying in the Spirit

*Be anxious for nothing, but in everything by prayer
and supplication, with thanksgiving, let your requests
be made known to God; and the peace of God,
which surpasses all understanding, will guard
your hearts and minds through Christ Jesus.
~ Philippians 4:6-7*

How is your anxiety level? The greatest gift that God has given us to overcome fear, anxiety, confusion, and stress, is praying in tongues. People are so hungry for the supernatural; they believe in prophecy and healing, but speaking in tongues is still controversial. When I get prayer burdens and feelings of anxiety, I pray in the spirit (tongues).

The word "tongues," is an archaic English word for languages. This amazing gift is received with the Baptism in the Holy Spirit. John the Baptist said that Jesus would baptize with the Holy Spirit (see Matthew 3:11). Jesus told His disciples to wait in Jerusalem until they received the Baptism with the Holy Spirit (see Acts 1:5). Finally, when 120 of the disciples were praying in the Upper Room, the Holy Spirit fell upon them and they ALL began speaking in other tongues and prophesying (see Acts 2:1-4). This pattern of people receiving the infilling of the Holy Spirit and speaking in tongues became a normal sign throughout the book of Acts (see Acts 10:44-48, 19:1-6).

When you ask Jesus to baptize you with the Holy Spirit, you too will speak in tongues and have a prayer language to help you speak to God.

This is what a prayer language is for:

- Praying in tongues will build you up in your faith and inner man. You will become more spiritually sensitive. – Jude 20-21, 1 Corinthians 14:4
- You will be able to pray beyond your limited understanding; you will pray mysteries.
  – 1 Corinthians 14:2.
- God interprets what you pray and brings things to your mind. – 1 Corinthians 14:13-15.
- Praying and singing in tongues expands your vocabulary for worship. – 1 Corinthians 14:13-14, Colossians 3;16.
- Whenever you pray in tongues, you pray the perfect will of God because the Spirit is praying through you. – Romans 8:26-28.
- It's the instrument God gives for rest and refreshing. – Isaiah 28:11-13 cross-reference 1 Corinthians 14:20-22.

If you already have a prayer language and you feel anxiety or despondency coming upon you, pray in tongues until you sense God's peace and refreshing.

If you want more power to overcome, please say this prayer with me:

Dear Lord Jesus,
   I ask that you baptize me with your Holy Spirit. I love you and desire the power and person of the Holy Spirit to help me to be a better witness for Christ and overcome. I now speak in tongues by faith believing that You will enable me.
   Amen

Supernatural Joy

You know it is God's will for you to be Baptized with the Holy Spirit (see Luke 11:13). Therefore, you must believe that you received it when you asked, with sincerity, and begin speaking in tongues by faith. It's a partnership; you speak and the Holy Spirit gives you utterance.

Therefore I say to you, whatever things you ask when you pray, believe that you receive them, and you will have them.
~ Mark 11:24

And they were all filled with the Holy Spirit and began to speak with other tongues, as the Spirit gave them utterance.
~ Acts 2:4

If you then, being evil, know how to give good gifts to your children, how much more will your heavenly Father give the Holy Spirit to those who ask Him!
~ Luke 11:1

How to Know God Personally

The only way to have lasting joy is by knowing God. By "knowing God," I am not talking about knowing *about* God or having a knowledge *of* God from growing up in church. I am talking about knowing Him personally. I am talking about *being born again into a new life*.

And this is eternal life, that they may know You, the only true God, and Jesus Christ whom You have sent.
~ John 17:3

Only in Christianity can one know God and have a personal relationship with Him. In all other religions, their gods are unknowable. To have peace with God and to have His friendship, protection, and joy are the most valuable things in the universe. But how do you connect with God almighty? How do you have an assurance that you will go to heaven and have eternal life? Let me share with you four spiritual laws and how you can have peace with God.

1. The Human problem is sin. Sin is disobedience to a Holy God. When the first man Adam sinned, death, sickness, war, all injustice and evil came into the world. Because you and I were born with a disposition to sin, we are separated from a Holy God. We all have sinned in thought, words, and deeds. There are sins of commission (sins which we do and commit) and sins of omission (things that we omit to do but should do, like giving thanks to God). Our sin nature causes us to do terrible things to one another. If God stopped all sin, it would be judgment day and many are not ready to meet their God, are you? (see Romans 3:9-18)

> *For all have sinned and fall short of the glory of God.*
> *~ Romans 3:23*

2. Humanity has hope in Christ. Jesus took the punishment for our sins. We cannot earn our salvation and friendship with God. Although we are capable of good deeds, we can never be self-righteous. We can never be religious enough or smart enough to appease a most Holy God.

> *But we are all like an unclean thing, and all our righteousnesses are like filthy rags; We all fade as a leaf, And our iniquities, like the wind, Have taken us away.*
> *~ Isaiah 64:6*

What we could not do on our own, God did for us. He sent His Son to make a way and a bridge to Himself. Jesus paid the death penalty for your sin so that you could live. The death of a mere man could not be enough to appease the wrath of Almighty God. And God could not die, so God became a man, lived a sinless life, and died vicariously for you on the cross.

> *But God demonstrates His own love toward us, in that while we were still sinners, Christ died for us.*
> *~ Romans 5:8*

> *For the wages of sin is death, but the gift of God is eternal life in Christ Jesus our Lord.*
> *~ Romans 6:23*

3. The sinner's response. Confess and completely trust God. You must choose to receive this free gift from Him. You have a free will and can choose to reject God's offer of His friendship. What is your response to God's offer of peace, joy, friendship, and eternal life? (see John 1:12-13, 3:16-17)

> *If you confess with your mouth the Lord Jesus and believe in your heart that God has raised Him from the dead, you will be*

> *saved. For with the heart one believes unto righteousness, and with the mouth confession is made unto salvation.*
> ~ Romans 10:9-10

4. The result of salvation is peace and friendship with God (see Romans 8:1).

> *Therefore, having been justified by faith, we have peace with God through our Lord Jesus Christ.*
> ~ Romans 5:1

> *For the Scripture says, "Whoever believes on Him will not be put to shame." For there is no distinction between Jew and Greek, for the same Lord over all is rich to all who call upon Him. For "whoever calls on the name of the Lord shall be saved."*
> ~ Romans 10:11-13

> *No longer do I call you servants, for a servant does not know what his master is doing; but I have called you friends, for all things that I heard from My Father I have made known to you.*
> ~ John 15:15

If you are ready to turn (repent) from what you know is wrong and trust in Christ, please say this prayer.

Dear God,
I know that I'm a sinner, and I ask for Your forgiveness.
I believe Jesus Christ is Your Son. I believe that He died for my sin and that You raised Him to life again.
I want to trust Him as my Savior and follow Him as Lord from this day forward.
Guide my life and help me to do Your will.
I pray this in the name of Jesus, Amen.

If you said this prayer and meant it from your heart, congratulations! You have now begun an amazing adventure in a rich life with the protection and leading of Almighty God. You are now a new creation and everything has a new perspective. Your future looks good. What was impossible with man is now possible because God is with you.

Therefore, if anyone is in Christ, he is a new creation; old things have passed away; behold, all things have become new.
~ II Corinthians 5:17

But Jesus looked at them and said, "With men it is impossible, but not with God; for with God all things are possible."
~ Mark 10:27

To grow spiritually, it's important that you do three things:

1. Read your Bible and pray daily

As newborn babes, desire the pure milk of the word, that you may grow thereby, if indeed you have tasted that the Lord is gracious. Therefore, laying aside all malice, all deceit, hypocrisy, envy, and all evil speaking.
~ I Peter 2:1-3

Continue earnestly in prayer, being vigilant in it with thanksgiving.
~ Colossians 4:2

2. Find a good church where Christ is preached and taught; they can help you in understanding the Bible and to live for Christ.

And let us consider one another in order to stir up love and good works, not forsaking the assembling of ourselves together, as is the manner of some, but exhorting one another, and so much the more as you see the Day approaching.
~ Hebrews 10:24-25

3. Witness and share what good things God has done for you.

Let the redeemed of the Lord say so, Whom He has redeemed from the hand of the enemy.
~ Psalms 107:2

www.ingramcontent.com/pod-product-compliance
Lightning Source LLC
Chambersburg PA
CBHW071031080526
44587CB00015B/2572